SCIENCE **SPOTLIGHT**

CRIME-FIGHTING

IAN GRAHAM

EVANS BROTHERS LIMITED

DC013512

Evans Brothers Limited
2A Portman Mansions
Chiltern Street
London W1M 1LE

First published 1993

Printed in Hong Kong by Dah Hua Printing Co Ltd

ISBN 0 237 51295 5

Editor: Su Swallow
Designer: Neil Sayer
Production: Peter Thompson
Illustrations: Hardlines, Charlbury
Graeme Chambers

The author and publishers would like to thank Anne Holdsworth of The Forensic Science Society for her help in the preparation of this book.

Acknowledgements

For permission to reproduce copyright material the author and publishers gratefully acknowledge the following:

Cover (top and bottom) J.C. Revy, Science Photo Library **Page 4** (top left) The Hulton-Deutsch Collection (bottom) The Metropolitan Police Service **page 5** (middle) Frank Wiles, Mary Evans Picture Library (bottom) The Image Bank **page 6** (top) Martin Dohrn, Science Photo Library (bottom) The Metropolitan Police Service **page 7** (top) The Metropolitan Police Service (right) Mary Evans Picture Library **page 8** (top) Alfred Pasieka, The Image Bank (bottom) Foster & Freeman Ltd **page 9** Philippe Plailly, Science Photo Library **page 10** (top) JC Revy, Science Photo Library (bottom) Michael Gilbert, Science Photo Library **page 11** (top) Peter Menzel, Science Photo Library (bottom) James Holmes, Cellmark Diagnostics, Science Photo Library **page 12** (top) Sally Morgan, Ecoscene (bottom) RL Manuel, Oxford Scientific Films **page 13** (left) CNRI, Science Photo Library (right) Mary Evans Picture Library **page 14** (top) Horst Thanhaeuser, The Image Bank (bottom) Sally Morgan, Ecoscene **page 15** Foster & Freeman Ltd **page 16** Dr Jeremy Burgess, Science Photo Library **page 17** (top) Brown, Ecoscene (bottom) National Library of Medicine, Science Photo Library **page 19** (top left) Otto Rogge, NHPA (top right) Stephen Dalton, NHPA (middle left) Stephen Dalton, NHPA (middle right) Stephen Dalton, NHPA (bottom) L Campbell, NHPA **page 20** (top) Manfred Kage, Science Photo Library (bottom) Ronald Tom, Oxford Scientific Films **page 21** (top) Ronald Toms, Oxford Scientific Films (bottom) The Metropolitan Police Service **page 22** Adrienne Hart-Davis, Science Photo Library **page 23** Stephen Dalton, Oxford Scientific Films **page 24** (top) The Metropolitan Police Service (bottom) Sheila Terry, Science Photo Library **page 25** (right) Michel Tcherevkoff, The Image Bank (left) Dr Jeremy Burgess, Science Photo Library **page 26** (top) Jody Dole, The Image Bank (middle) Sally Morgan, Ecoscene **page 27** (top) Foster & Freeman Ltd **page 28** (top) Sheila Terry, Science Photo Library (bottom) Johannes Hofmann, Okapia, Oxford Scientific Films **page 29** Jerry Mason, Science Photo Library (bottom) E Hanumantha, NHPA **page 30** (middle) Geoff Tompkinson, Science Photo Library (bottom) Mary Evans Picture Library **page 32** The Metropolitan Police Service (bottom) Hicks Photographic Services **page 33** Hicks Photographic Services **page 34** (top) Sally Morgan, Ecoscene (bottom) Nicholas Foster, The Image Bank **page 35** (top) The Forensic Science Service (bottom) The Hulton-Deutsch Collection **page 36** The Metropolitan Police Service **page 37** (top) Labat/Lanceau, Jerrican, Science Photo Library (bottom) The Hulton-Deutsch Collection **page 38** (top) Michel Tcherevkoff, The Image Bank (bottom) The Metropolitan Police Service **page 39** Jerry Young **page 40** Jerry Young **page 41** Jerry Young **pages 42 and 43** The Metropolitan Police Service

Contents

Introduction

SCIENTISTS BELIEVE that it is impossible for someone to commit a crime without leaving something behind or taking something away with them. If these traces of evidence can be found, they may provide the proof needed to bring the criminal to justice. They may take the form of fingerprints, hairs, fibres from clothing, tiny traces of chemicals, documents, bullets or fragments of glass. This evidence is collected and studied by forensic scientists. Forensic means 'applied to the law'.

A fingerprint expert at work in the 1940s. Today, modern technology has speeded up the matching process.

A forensic scientist looks at a DNA fingerprint (see page 10).

SCIENCE IS APPLIED TO CRIME-FIGHTING more now than ever before. As people find new ways to commit crimes and new ways to cover their tracks, scientists develop new techniques for linking suspects with their crimes and proving their guilt.

Old techniques are constantly being improved so that they can be applied to smaller and smaller traces of materials. In the past, there was no way of identifying a criminal unless he or she was caught 'red-handed' – that is, actually committing the crime. If the criminal got away unseen, there was no way of proving who had done the deed. Nowadays the story is very different. Forensic scientists have an enormous variety of tests, techniques and equipment that enable them to collect the tiniest pieces of evidence and identify them. The range of their work is so great that any one scientist could not possibly be expert in all of it. So, forensic scientists often specialise in one branch of their work. There are specialists in documents, firearms, fires, explosives, chemicals, poisons and handwriting. Several specialists may be needed to collect all the evidence from the scene of a crime or from a suspect.

Other scientific specialists who are not full-time forensic scientists are often called in to help when their skills are needed. Psychologists can give the police a description of the type of person they are seeking. Insect specialists, called cntomologists, advise on insects found during an inquiry, and so on. All of these scientists work together as a team to try to reveal the story of a crime that might otherwise remain secret. **Crime-fighting** looks at the work of forensic scientists and explains some of the methods they use.

A Victorian detective

WHEN THE INVESTIGATION of crimes by the police was still in its infancy and before forensic scientists as we know them today existed, one famous figure was already able to solve crimes by 'reading' clues left by the criminal. The ways in which he collected facts and worked out what they meant was very similar to the methods that

police officers and forensic scientists use today. He was Sherlock Holmes. Many people still believe that Sherlock Holmes was a real person, but actually he never existed. He was invented by the author, Sir Arthur Conan Doyle. Doyle's stories about Holmes and his assistant Dr Watson first

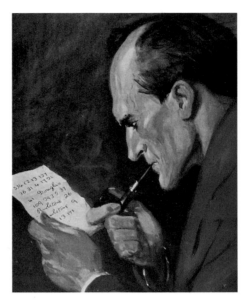

Sherlock Holmes

appeared in the *Strand* magazine in 1891 and they continued until 1925. Holmes lived at 221B Baker Street, London, a real address which is visited by people from all over the world.

Plays and films about the famous detective and the cases he solved are still popular today.

HISTORY SPOTLIGHT

HISTORY SPOTLIGHT boxes focus on an important technique, a piece of equipment or a key figure in the history of some of the topics.

Modern forensic science can be traced back to the middle of the 19th century. By the 1850s, policemen were beginning to look for clues at the scene of a crime that might lead them to the person responsible. Scientists began to take an interest in the new field of criminology, too, and forensic science was born. The new science was pioneered in France, where the first forensic science laboratory was set up in 1910. The first British and American forensic science labs were set up in the 1930s.

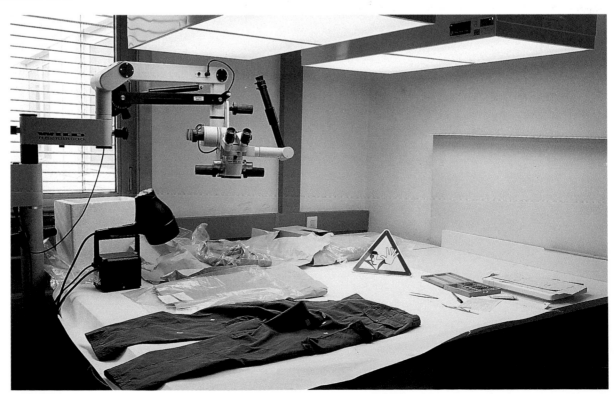

Pieces of evidence gathered from the scene of a crime.

Fingerprints

EACH PERSON IS A UNIQUE COMBINATION of hundreds of different factors – size, shape, eye colour, hair colour, skin colour and so on. Yet until 1900 there was no scientific way of using any of this information to identify someone. Crime-fighters needed one simple measurement or mark that would be unique to each individual. The fingerprint is just such a mark. It is not the only means of identification, but it has become the most widespread. It is used all over the world.

Fingerprints provide some of the best clues to a person's identity.

FINGERPRINTS ARE NORMALLY INVISIBLE, so the first task at the scene of a crime is to find them. The invisible prints are called latent prints and the process of making them visible is called developing. Forensic scientists normally develop latent prints by brushing a fine aluminium 'dusting powder' over places where prints are most likely to be found – around door handles, drawers, window catches and stair rails, for example. The fine powder is trapped by the lines of sticky, oily sweat left behind by the fingers. Black powder is used on pale surfaces to make the prints stand out more clearly. They can then be photographed.

Fingerprints can even be taken away to the laboratory. They are removed by sticking a piece of clear adhesive tape over them. When the tape is peeled away again, the powder pattern of the print sticks to the tape. The tape can then be stuck on to a piece of card and taken away for closer examination.

Dusting for fingerprints

Classifying fingerprints

AN IDENTIFICATION SYSTEM has to work quickly. It would obviously take far too long to compare fingerprints found at the scene of a crime with all the prints held on file. London's Metropolitan Police, for example, has about four million fingerprint records stored in its computer files. The Federal Bureau of Investigation (FBI) in the United States has more than

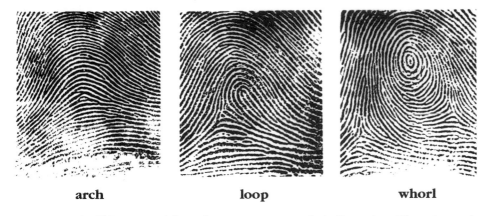

arch   **loop**   **whorl**

Most people (65 per cent) have loop patterns on their fingertips. Three in ten have whorls and the remaining five per cent have arches.

An arch fingerprint with the points used to check a person's identity. The points may be where ridges come together, end or divide in two.

HISTORY SPOTLIGHT

In the 1870s, photographs were used to keep records of criminals. But there was no way of classifying people or their photographs. A French detective, Alphonse Bertillon (1853-1914), tackled this problem by classifying people according to their measurements. When anyone was brought in for questioning by the Paris police, Bertillon took measurements from the suspect. To these he added two photographs and a description. The scientific name for the system is anthropometry, but it became known as the Bertillon system. When a suspect was arrested Bertillon took his measurements and compared them with those on file. If he found a match, the photographs and description would confirm the identification. But it was a very complicated system and its success depended on the measurements being accurate to within a millimetre. By the 1890s, a much simpler and more reliable system called dactyloscopy (fingerprinting) was being developed. It replaced the Bertillon system in the early 1900s.

80 million criminal fingerprint records, and millions of non-criminal records from people such as government employees. Fortunately, fingerprints are classified (divided) into different types according to their pattern. This reduces the search time.

The basic system was developed by Sir Edward Henry, the Inspector General of Police in Bengal, in 1900. It was so successful that it was adopted by police forces all over the world. According to the Henry classification system, all prints fall into one of three basic types – loops, whorls and arches – named after the pattern of lines on the fingertip. Each of these groups is sub-divided into smaller groups according to differences in the pattern detail within each group – the arch pattern, for example, may be plain or 'tented'. An unknown print found at the scene of a crime and a known print held on file are accepted by courts of law as coming from the same person if they are identical at a minimum of 12 points.

Modern fingerprinting methods

A computer image of a fingerprint

FINGERPRINTS HAVE BEEN USED to help identify criminals for almost 100 years. In that time, many new scientific research methods have been developed. Some of them have provided scientists with new ways of finding and developing fingerprints.

This portable light source can be used in the laboratory or at the scene of the crime to show up fingerprints. The scientist wears goggles to protect her eyes from the very intense light.

THE TRADITIONAL WAY OF DUSTING surfaces for fingerprints is still used most of the time. In most cases it works very well, but sometimes different methods are needed. Forensic scientists can now use a small portable laser to look for fingerprints. The scientist 'paints' the scene of the crime with the laser beam. As the beam sweeps across doors, walls and furniture, any fingerprints present on them glow because they are fluorescent. Some atoms in the print absorb the laser light, and then release it again in the form of a burst of light. All of these tiny flashes combine to make the whole print glow when the laser beam hits it.

The technique of laser-sweeping enables large areas to be searched quickly, and prints in odd places can be found. Dusting the same surfaces with powder would take much longer and prints in unlikely places could be missed altogether. Prints found by a laser can also be dusted with a fluorescent powder to make them show up even more clearly so they can be photographed.

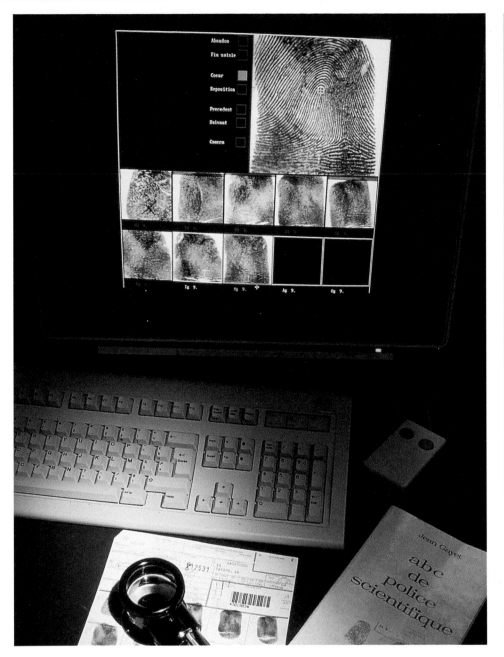

HISTORY SPOTLIGHT

THE WORD LASER is formed from the initials of Light Amplification by Stimulated Emission of Radiation. It describes how a laser works – by forcing, or stimulating, atoms to emit intense (amplified) radiation in the form of light. The story of the laser dates back to 1917, when Einstein showed that, in theory at least, atoms could be made to produce radiation.

In 1954, three American scientists – Gordon, Zeigler and Townes – produced an instrument based on Einstein's work, called a maser (Microwave Amplification by Stimulated Emission of Radiation). It produced a beam of radio waves from atoms of ammonia gas.

By the end of the 1950s, scientists were looking for a way to make a maser that could produce a beam of light. Theodore Maiman made the first optical masers, in 1960. Soviet scientists developed similar devices at the same time. Optical masers became known as lasers in 1965.

A 'digitiser' (at the bottom of the picture) is used to convert old paper copies of criminals' fingerprint records into computer records.

Prints on paper

IT IS DIFFICULT TO DETECT prints on absorbent surfaces, such as paper, because the oil and sweat of the print sinks into the surface. These prints have to be developed chemically. A technique called fuming is sometimes used.

Fuming involves blowing chemical fumes over likely surfaces. The fumes react chemically with sweat or oils in any fingerprints and they change colour, revealing the print. Although the technique is old, new chemicals are still being tried to find the best one for developing clear images of prints. Iodine has been used as a fuming chemical for many years. Fingerprints turn yellow-brown when they are exposed to iodine vapour. But iodine is not the ideal chemical to use because it is poisonous and it does not always develop prints clearly.

In the early 1980s another type of fuming chemical was found, by accident. A new type of glue popularly known as 'superglue' had become available. Forensic scientists discovered that invisible fingerprints on an object turned white if the object was left near something that had been repaired with superglue. One of the chemicals in the vapour given off by the glue sticks to the print. As more and more glue vapour settles on the pattern of the print and hardens, the print itself becomes visible as a white mark.

Genetic fingerprints

THE HUMAN BODY is composed of millions of microscopic cells. Each cell contains a unique code, the genetic code that determines what we look like and how we develop. The code takes the form of long strings of molecules called DNA. No two people have identical DNA unless they are identical twins.

A TECHNIQUE FOR READING GENETIC CODES was developed in the 1980s. DNA profiling, or genetic fingerprinting, was quickly taken up by the police and forensic scientists as a way of linking suspected criminals with their crimes.

A computer image of a short section of DNA

Making genetic fingerprints

THE PROCESS OF MAKING A DNA profile may begin with a scrap of stained clothing found at the scene of the crime. A tuft of hair or droplets of body fluids such as blood can be used too. The material

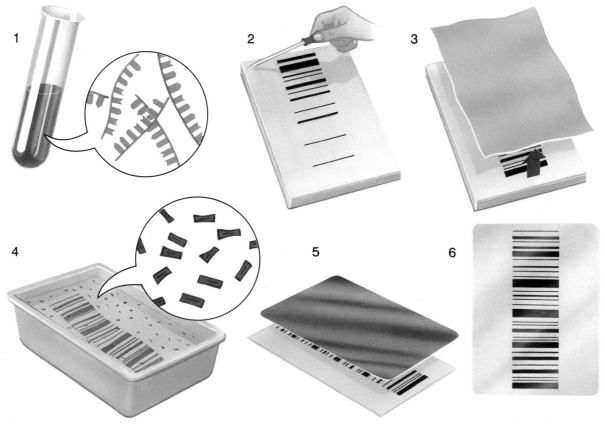

To make a genetic fingerprint, DNA is extracted from the body fluid (1), broken into fragments and placed on a layer of jelly (2). An electric current forces the fragments to separate into (invisible) bands, which are transferred to a nylon sheet (3). The sheet is placed in a bath and radioactive DNA is added (4). Photographic film is laid on the sheet (5) and developed to reveal the 'fingerprint' (6).

is soaked so that any body cells in the stain come away from the cloth and into the liquid. The cells are then broken open to let out the long threads of DNA. These are treated chemically to cut them into tiny pieces. A blob of these DNA fragments is then placed at one end of a layer of special jelly.

When an electric current is passed through the jelly from one end to the other, the pieces of DNA move through the jelly in the direction of the electric current. The process is called electrophoresis. The shorter pieces of DNA can move through the jelly more easily than the longer pieces. After a while, the DNA separates out into bands according to the size of the fragments, although at this stage the bands are invisible.

The pattern of DNA bands then has to be transferred to a nylon sheet. The nylon sheet is then treated to make the DNA

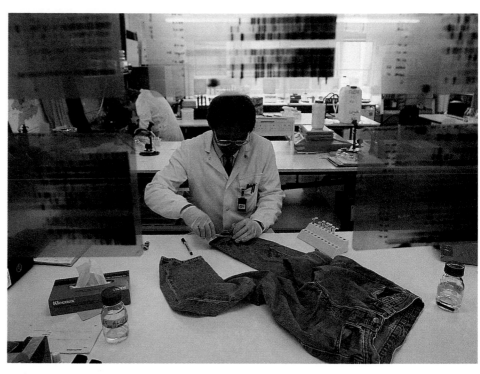

A forensic scientist takes a blood sample from a stained pair of jeans. DNA from the sample will be used to provide a DNA fingerprint.

radioactive. When photographic film is laid on top of the nylon sheet for a while and then developed chemically, the bands of DNA appear as dark stripes of different thicknesses on the film.

A scientist compares DNA fingerprints on a lightbox.

If the pattern of bands produced by cells found at the scene of the crime exactly matches the pattern made by cells collected from the suspect, then the body cells from both samples must belong to the suspect and he or she must have been present at the scene of the crime. With a good sample that is rich in DNA, the chance of two people producing the same genetic fingerprint is only one in 2.7 million, which is good enough for a court of law. However, people who are related do have similarities in their DNA. The chance of two related people producing the same genetic fingerprint is as high as one in 200. If there is not enough good quality DNA material for a reliable test, the chance of two people producing the same genetic fingerprint could rise to one in 50. So the value of DNA profiling depends on the circumstances of the case.

Tell-tale teeth

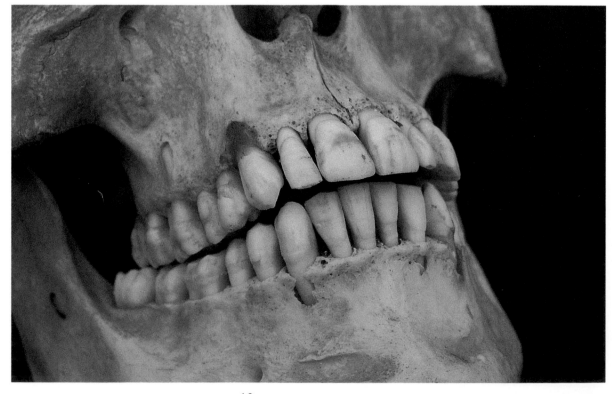

A bite mark on a piece of cheese

FINGERPRINTS AND DNA PROFILING ('genetic fingerprints') can often prove someone's identity beyond any reasonable doubt. But occasionally other methods have to be used. The mouth contains its own 'print' that can identify its owner. Teeth and dental records are sometimes used to identify a criminal.

NO TWO PEOPLE have exactly the same size, shape and numbers of teeth. However, teeth have never been used as a common identification system in the same way as fingerprints because, unlike fingerprints, 'dental prints' can change. Over the years, teeth may become worn down or be lost due to disease and decay. Fillings and dentures would also alter a dental print. So the teeth of a person of 20 would almost certainly look very different from the teeth of the same person at 60. Despite this, teeth can still often help to prove identity.

A peckish burglar who takes a mouthful of food at the scene of his crime may leave behind valuable evidence for the forensic scientist. When hard foods are bitten into, the remaining piece of the food retains a 'print' of the teeth that bit into them. If photographs or casts of the teeth marks are compared to a suspect, a match between them can prove the burglar's guilt. The scientist must record the teeth marks quickly, because they will shrink and change shape if the food is allowed to dry out.

Teeth are also very useful

A full set of teeth in a human skull

A computer image of pairs of chromosomes from a man. The nucleus of each human cell contains 23 pairs. Only men have Y chromosomes.

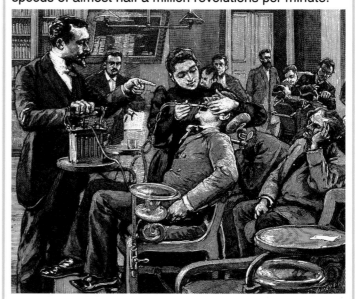
for identifying unknown bodies. If a body has lain undiscovered for a very long time, there may only be bones left, making identification all the more difficult. The size of the teeth can suggest whether the body is that of a man or a woman. Men generally have larger teeth than women. The state of the teeth – how much they are decayed or worn – can help in estimating the person's age. If any pulp (the material inside the tooth) is still present it can be stained with a fluorescent chemical that glows when a light is shone on it. The blobs of tissue that carry the cells' genetic code take up the chemical stain in a a special way. The genetic code is contained in chromosomes, and it is only the Y chromosomes that become stained. Women do not have any Y chromosomes. So if any chromosomes glow when a light is shone on the stained tooth pulp, the tooth must have come from a man.

It may be possible to match dental work such as fillings or dentures with dental records of missing persons. If there is anything odd about the teeth, such as gaps or badly-shaped teeth, comparing a photograph of a missing person's smile in life to the teeth in the skull of an unknown body may be enough to prove the identity of the body. The branch of forensic science that deals with teeth is called forensic odontology.

Data-discs on teeth

IN FUTURE, TEETH may be even more useful as a means of identification. In 1986, American dentists began fixing a pinhead-sized disc to an upper molar of each patient. The tiny disc carries a 12-digit code that identifies the patient. If a body with one of these discs on a tooth is found, it can be identified easily by telephoning the dental register.

Tools and treads

A footprint in wet sand

A tyre tread in damp soil

WHEN A BURGLAR breaks into a building or a vehicle, he leaves marks behind on any windows, or doors that he had to break or force open. If he drives over soft ground, the tyres of his vehicle leave marks in the ground. And his shoes or boots may leave footprints in places. A lot can be learned from the marks a burglar leaves behind.

ONE SCREWDRIVER or chisel may look the same as many others, but each one gets knocked and scratched in different ways in its lifetime. The marks on its blade are almost as good as a fingerprint for identifying it later. If a tool-mark is found it is photographed. The forensic scientist then presses a pad of quick-setting plastic on to it. When the plastic sets and is peeled away, an impression of the mark is moulded into the plastic. Tools found by the police can be compared with this. The tool used to make the mark will match the plastic cast exactly.

Tyre treads

WHEN A VEHICLE is driven over soft ground, its tyre tread patterns are pressed into the ground. The tread is designed to squeeze water out from beneath the tyre so that the tyre grips the road in the rain. By examining the marks, a forensic scientist can tell in which direction the vehicle was travelling and whether it kept moving or stopped in one place for a while. Like tools, tyres acquire unique marks. Cuts and embedded stones give each tyre its own 'fingerprint'.

A tread mark can be photographed and lifted just like a fingerprint. When the tread pattern is photographed, the flashgun is held to one side so that the peaks and troughs cast shadows and show up the pattern more clearly. A ruler is laid alongside the print so that accurate measurements can be taken from the photograph. Lifting a tyre tread print is not quite as easy as lifting a fingerprint. A 'fence' of foil or card is made around the tread pattern. Then quick-setting

A portable shoeprint lifter (below) which lifts indistinct dustmarks of shoeprints. Lifting film is placed over the shoeprint and charged to attract the dust. The dustmarks can then be removed and photographed in a studio. The lifter can lift prints from difficult surfaces, including paper and cardboard (right).

dental plaster is poured in. The ground may have been made water-resistant first, by spraying it with a fluid such as shellac, to stop the plaster from soaking down into it. When the plaster has set hard, it provides a permanent record of the tyre tread. Shoes often leave marks in soft ground in the same way as a tyre tread. And the shoe print can be lifted in the same way, with plaster. Scientists can learn something about the suspect and his movements from footprints. Feet and shoes may also leave prints on smooth polished floors. They are more difficult to see, but they can provide important clues about a suspect's size, weight and movements.

HISTORY SPOTLIGHT

PLASTER CASTS of footprints were used to prove someone's guilt as long ago as 1786. Footprints were found in soft ground near the scene of a murder. Plaster casts of the prints were made and compared to the boots worn by a suspect. The casts and the boots matched exactly. The suspect was found guilty of the crime and executed.

Comparing two footprints under a powerful lens fitted with a bright fluorescent lamp

Soil, seeds and pollen

NATURE IS OFTEN A GREAT HELP to the forensic scientist. The seeds of some plants are often found only in certain places and at certain times of the year. If they are carried away on the clothing of a suspect or the victim of a crime, they can provide valuable evidence.

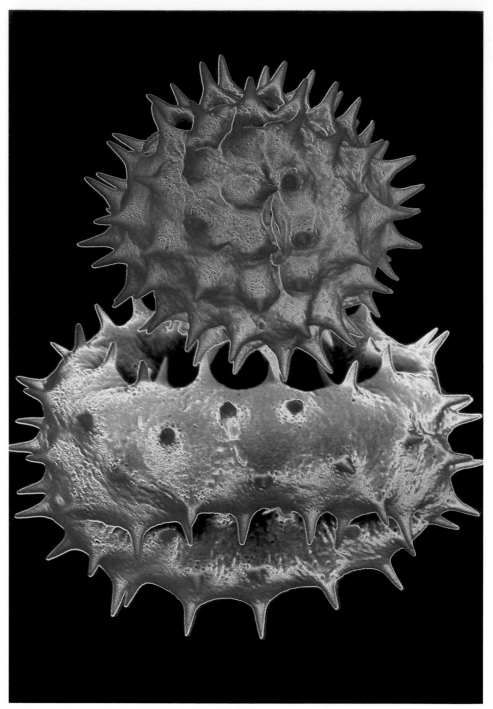

A magnified computer image of pollen grains from a marigold flower. The barbs may hook on to the body of an insect – or a person's clothes.

Pollen falling from the catkin of an alder tree

ANY CRIMINAL WHO WALKS over a field or garden, squeezes past a hedge, is knocked to the ground in a struggle or goes anywhere near plants stands a good chance of picking up seeds, flower petals, pollen or other pieces of vegetation on their clothes. And it may help to prove that a suspect could have been at or near the scene of a crime. If, for example, a house is burgled by someone who had to stand in a patch of dandelions to break a window, the presence of dandelion seeds in the suspect's clothes could be very difficult for him or her to explain. If the plants had been sprayed with weedkiller the same day and traces of the same weedkiller is found on the

HISTORY SPOTLIGHT

THE USE OF NATURAL CLUES in forensic science depends on the ability to classify plants and their seeds and pollen accurately. The principles that scientists use for naming and classifying plants (and animals) today were established by the Swedish botanist Carl von Linné (1707-78), who is better known by the Latin form of his name, Carolus Linnaeus. He gave each plant a name with two parts – the system is therefore known as binomial nomenclature. The first name is the plant's genus and the second is its species. Plants that are similar and which can breed easily with each other are placed in the same species, and species that share common features are placed in the same genus. For example, the primrose is Primula vulgaris and the oxslip, which is a different species of primula, is Primula elatior. The Latin names are chosen to describe some feature of the plant. Primula comes from the Latin word *primus*, meaning first, because of the primula's early flowering habit. Vulgaris means common, because the plant is very widespread, and elatior means taller, because the oxslip is a tall form of primula.

The Latin name for the white poppy – Papaver somniferum – is shown on this 19th century drawing.

suspect's clothes, the case against him or her is strengthened even more.

Soil, too, can yield vital clues. If, for example, a footprint is found in soft earth outside a burgled house, it may not show enough detail to prove conclusively that it was made by a similar shoe found in the house of a suspect. It may be an average size of a popular shoe that many people wear. However, if traces of the soil from the scene of the crime are found on the shoes' soles, that could be more difficult for the suspect to explain.

Soil is a rich mixture of chemicals, rocky particles of different sizes, plant material and microscopic organisms. Some soils are acidic, others are alkaline and many are neutral. They contain a wide range of different chemicals – chlorides, phosphates, carbonates, sulphates and nitrates – in different proportions. A close match between the soil found on the shoe and soil at the scene of a crime cannot prove that the soil on the suspect's shoe must have come from the scene of the crime – other nearby fields and gardens probably have a similar soil type. But the match would add one more piece of evidence that the suspect has to explain. If natural clues like these may be of use, a forensic scientist will take the suspect's clothes to the laboratory and clean them by brushing, vacuuming and using sticky tape to remove particles. The scientist examines all the material collected under a microscope, and lists all the seeds and pollen present. And by carrying out simple chemical tests on soil traces, the soil type can be added to the list. Even if the scientist has not visited the scene of the crime, he or she may be able to tell the police what types of plants are growing nearby and what sort of soil is present.

Insect helpers

DETECTIVES need to know when a person died to help them to work out what happened to him or her. Knowing the time of death accurately can eliminate some suspects and bring others under suspicion. Sometimes, forensic scientists enlist the help of insects.

WHEN ANY LIVING CREATURE dies, a series of natural changes takes place. The three most obvious changes that occur in human bodies in the hours immediately after death are known as algor mortis, livor mortis and rigor mortis, which mean the temperature, colour and stiffness of death.

When someone dies, chemical activity ceases and the body begins to cool down at the rate of about one degree per hour. So the temperature of a body can be used to estimate when someone died, provided that the surroundings in which the body is found are taken into account. A hot room or a chilly winter's day will alter the body's natural rate of cooling.

The colour of a body is important. Blood is normally pumped around the body by the heart. When the heart stops, the blood sinks to the lowest part of the body. After a while, the red blood cells begin to break down and leak through the walls of the blood vessels into the surrounding tissues. The red colour of the blood begins to appear on the skin. If a body is moved some time after death, perhaps from lying on its left side to its right, this colour change will not be at the lowest part of the body any more – a very suspicious circumstance.

The changes that occur after death also cause a stiffness in the muscles, which increases and spreads over the whole body in about 12 hours and then gradually goes away again. Rigor mortis is completely gone after about 36 hours. So any stiffness in the body helps to pinpoint the time when death occurred.

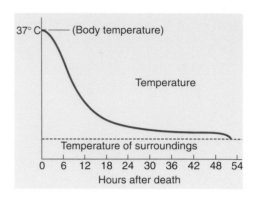

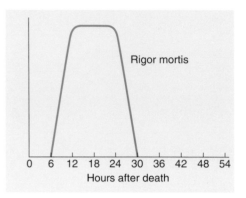

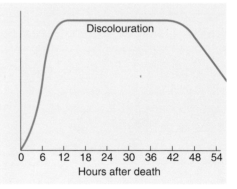

Fly clocks

FLIES CAN HELP the forensic scientists trying to estimate how long a body has lain undiscovered. When any living creature dies, organisms ranging from microscopic fungi and bacteria to worms and larger animals look upon it as a source of food. A human body is no different. It, too, falls prey to all of these organisms and animals. It may be an unpleasant thought, but it is a natural event, and as it

A bluebottle lays
its eggs on a
dead rat.

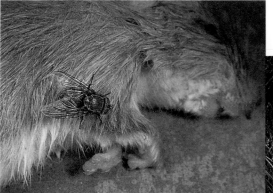

These bluebottle eggs will soon hatch into larvae.

Bluebottle larvae

A bluebottle hatches out of its
pupa case, only two or three
weeks after the egg was laid.

happens it can be useful to
forensic scientists.

Flies are particularly helpful.
Some of them, such as
bluebottles, seek out dead
animals on which to lay their
eggs. The eggs hatch within a
day or two into tiny larvae
which feed on the body.

The fly larvae grow by
moulting – throwing off each
skin as it becomes too small.
Each stage is called an instar.
Different species of flies go
through different numbers of
instars before the larvae change
into a pupa. This is similar to a

caterpillar's chrysalis. Within a
few days, the larva inside its
pupa case develops into an
adult fly. The whole process
from egg to adult takes two or
three weeks. The stage the
insects reach by the time a dead
body is found enables insect
specialists called entomologists
to count back the days to when
the eggs must have been laid. A
body, whether it is a mouse or a
man, does not lie for very long
before flies discover it and lay
their eggs. The unsuspecting
insects act like a clock for the
forensic scientist.

HISTORY SPOTLIGHT

THERE IS A CASE on record of wasps
helping to fix the time of
someone's death. By the time the
body was found, it was just a
skeleton. It was obviously at least
a year old, but how old? Five
years? Ten years? Twenty years?
Luckily for the scientists, a colony
of wasps had set up home in the
skull. From the state of the nest,
entomologists could estimate the
year in which the wasps had
started building it. And the body
must have been lying in the same
spot for a year before that to
reach a state that enabled the
wasps to move in. This enabled
the police to search the right year
of their missing persons' records
and to avoid wasting time
searching through records for
earlier and later years.

A wasp's nest in an attic

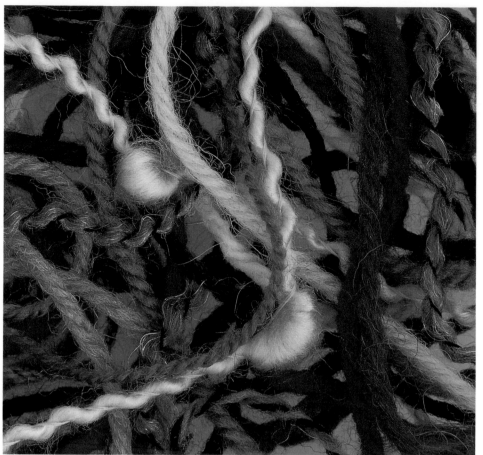
Woollen threads

Hairs and fibres

WE ARE CONSTANTLY DROPPING hair from our bodies and fibres from our clothes. It is almost impossible for a criminal and his victim to meet and touch without some hairs or fibres from one falling or rubbing off on to the other.

WHEN THE POLICE close in on a suspect, his clothes, especially clothes that fit a witness's description of the criminal, are taken away for examination. Strips of sticky tape are pressed all over them. Loose fibres stick to the tape, which is then examined under a microscope. Any fibres that do not belong to the clothes themselves may have been picked up from the scene of the crime, perhaps from the clothes worn by the victim or from carpets or curtains at the scene of the crime. And by examining fibres collected from the victim of a crime or from property seized by the police, scientists may be able to tell the police what sort of material they may have come from. In one case, a drug dealer shed so many fibres from a rug into his illegal packages that forensic scientists who

examined the packages were able to describe the tartan pattern on the rug to police officers!

The fibres of different materials look quite different under a microscope. The first step is to try to match fibres from the scene of the crime with fibres found in the suspect's clothes or car. Any fibres that seem to have come from the same place can then be analysed chemically to ensure that they really do match.

One method of analysing fibres is called spectro-photometry. White light is shone through the fibres. The dyes in the fibres absorb some wavelengths (colours) of light more than others. The light is then split into a spectrum of the separate colours that it contains by an instrument called a spectroscope. The intensities of the individual colours can then be measured by a second instrument, the spectrophotometer. It can even measure invisible infra-red radiation from the fibres. Different types of fibres produce different spectra.

Another method used for fibre analysis is thin-layer chromatography. It also works by splitting up the coloured dyes in artificial fibres into their separate colours, but in a different way. First, the dye is dissolved out of the fibres. Spots of the solution containing the dye are placed on a sheet of glass coated with silica gel, a kind of jelly, and allowed to dry. The sheet is then stood up on end with one edge sitting in a small tank of solvent. The solvent rises up through the gel by capillary action, just as water rises up into kitchen paper. When the solvent reaches the spots of dye, it keeps going, carrying the dye with it. Some colours are made up of smaller molecules than others. Smaller molecules are carried through the gel more easily than larger molecules and so they are carried farther. After a time, the dye has separated out into a series of coloured bands. Each band contains a different chemical compound. If the fibres have been coloured with a complicated or rare dye, the chromatography pattern on the glass can be almost as good as a fingerprint for matching fibres taken from a suspect with fibres collected from the scene of a crime.

It is not quite so easy to match hairs, because there are fewer types of hair than types of manufactured fibres. Even so, it is quite easy to see the difference between animal hairs and human hairs, and between hair from the head and from other parts of the body, when they are examined under a microscope. By looking at the hair roots, it is also possible to tell whether the hair fell out or was pulled out. And there may be other features that make it possible to match hair samples, such as colour and the use of bleaches and hair dyes.

Infra-red spectrophotometry

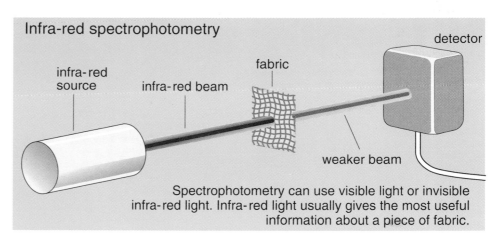

infra-red source

infra-red beam

fabric

detector

weaker beam

Spectrophotometry can use visible light or invisible infra-red light. Infra-red light usually gives the most useful information about a piece of fabric.

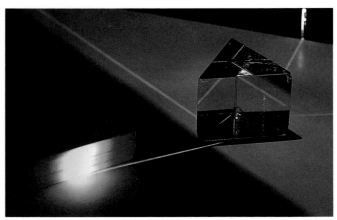
Thin-layer chromatography

As the solvent rises up through the gel, the dye separates out into its different chemical compounds.

Bits and pieces

WHEN A CRIME IS COMMITTED things often become broken. A window may be smashed to gain entry to a building. A car's paintwork may be scraped if it strikes something in the rush to get away. Forensic scientists are expert at finding the smallest fragments of material left behind after such events and analysing them.

A forensic scientist collects evidence from a broken window.

Stress patterns in glass fragments

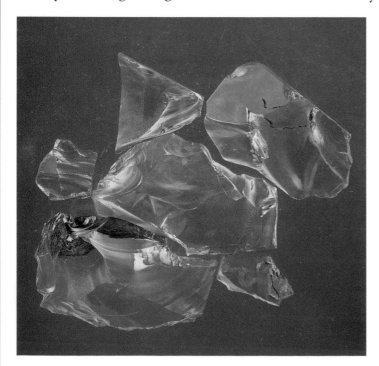

GLASS IS OFTEN BROKEN during a crime. It may be a window, smashed to let a burglar into a building. It may be a milk bottle knocked over accidentally. It may be a car's headlamp, broken when the car hit something. When glass shatters, the pieces can be sent flying over a wide area. And it is possible for the criminal to leave the scene with tiny slivers of glass caught in his clothes. If those pieces of glass can be found, it may be possible to match them with the broken glass found at the scene of the crime. If the broken window or bottle is reconstructed (stuck together again), the piece collected from the suspect may fit the glass jig-saw perfectly. As a double check, stress marks in the glass, called striations, which are caused by the intense heat used to manufacture the glass, should also match from one piece to another.

The ability of glass to bend light, called its refractive index, varies from one type of glass to another. Forensic scientists measure and compare the refractive index of glass at the scene of the crime and any glass fragments found on a

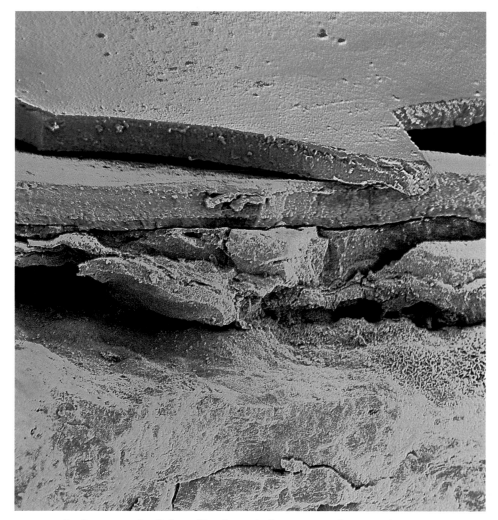

A magnified image of a flake of bodywork from a car, showing three paint colours. The yellow at the bottom is rust.

HISTORY SPOTLIGHT

WHEN A SHOPKEEPER was killed by being hit with a bottle, a forensic scientist painstakingly reconstructed the bottle from the hundreds of glass fragments found nearby. Weeks later, a tiny sliver of glass was found by vacuuming furniture in the home of a suspect. It was a perfect fit in the reconstructed bottle. The glass proved something that the suspect's fingerprints, which were also found at the scene, could not prove – that the suspect had not just visited the scene of the crime but was present at the scene when the crime was committed, because that is the only way that glass from the murder weapon could have been carried away by the suspect.

A scientist could reconstruct this panel of glass from the tiny fragments.

suspect's clothes to investigate whether they may have come from the same source.

Fragments of other materials can be carried away from a crime. When a car strikes something, or someone, tiny flakes of paint may be chipped off it. If paint flakes are found, the scientist can look at them edge-on under a microscope and see the different layers of paint in the flake. A car can have more than a dozen layers of paint. The particular colours and order of the layers are different for different makes and models of cars. Scientists can look up this paint 'fingerprint' in a computerised database to find out the make, year and of course colour of car that the paint came from. If paint flakes found on an object or victim match paint taken from a damaged car, then the suspect car must have struck the object or the victim. In the same way, flakes of paint or wallpaper scraped away as a burglar breaks into a building may stick to his clothes or to the tools used to force doors and windows open.

The pieces of material carried away from the scene of a crime by someone can be so small that they can only be seen clearly through a microscope. The scientist collects them by vacuuming the suspect's car or pressing sticky tape all over the suspect's clothing. The contents of the vacuum cleaner bag and anything sticking to the tape are examined under a microscope for anything that might have been picked up at the scene of the crime. The contents of the suspect's own vacuum cleaner bag are also frequently examined by scientists in case the criminal has tried to remove evidence by vacuuming his home or car.

Documents

US dollar bills being printed

CRIMES OFTEN INVOLVE DOCUMENTS of one sort or another. A kidnapper may send a ransom note. A blackmailer may write to his victim. Entries in a diary may help to reveal a missing person's movements. Scribbled notes on a scrap of paper may hold vital clues.

Entry and exit stamps in a passport

THERE ARE SEVERAL ways of examining documents to find out if they are genuine and have not been altered in any way. Documents fall into three broad categories – handwritten, typewritten and printed. Handwritten notes and letters are most commonly involved in criminal cases. A graphologist, a handwriting expert, may be able to tell whether a note is genuine from the way the letters are formed. Handwriting normally flows smoothly. Any sign that the writer has stopped and started or gone back over some letters to change their shape may indicate that the note is a forgery.

Most of a written note may be genuine, but it may have been altered. Amounts on cheques and dates on official documents may have been changed. If the police suspect that this may have happened, the ink on a document can be tested. Different inks respond to light differently. The document is lit by a series of lights, especially infra-red and ultraviolet. Lasers may be used too. Any alterations to a document will have been done in an ink that matches the colour of the original, but it is unlikely to match the original ink in every aspect of its chemical make-up. Different chemicals absorb and reflect different wavelengths (colours) of light in different ways. If a document has been altered, the alteration will show itself by glowing differently from the rest of the document under the test lights. Alterations to printed documents can be detected in the same way.

Typewritten documents can be almost as distinctive and individual as a sample of handwriting. In time, typewriter keys become worn, bent and damaged. Faced with a typewritten note and a selection of typewriters taken from suspects' homes and offices, a document specialist will be able say which typewriter was used to produce the document. The paper on which a note is written or typed may be as useful as the message on it. Paper linked to a crime may be matched with paper found in a suspect's home. The torn edge of a ransom note may fit with a torn edge on a writing pad belonging to the suspect. A message may be made from letters torn out of a newspaper. A newspaper found in a suspect's home with pieces torn out could be difficult to explain!

Banknotes are among the most valuable documents we have. It is important that they should be as difficult as possible to copy or forge. They are therefore often printed using special inks on special paper. The paper may have a watermark, a mark impressed on the paper when it is made and only visible when the paper is held up to the light.

The paper may also have a metal strip running through it. Different countries use different security measures, but all banknotes have a very intricate design to make it as difficult as possible for anyone to copy.

This equipment allows scientists to detect document forgery. It reveals differences in dyes and pigments.

The ESDA test

WHEN SOMETHING IS WRITTEN on the top page of a pad, the next few sheets underneath carry an impression of whatever was written on the top sheet. And it stays there even when the original note has been torn off. A deep impression can sometimes be seen by shining a light across the pad at an angle, to throw the impression into shadow. Lighter impressions can be read by a test called the ESDA test – Electro-Static Document Analysis.

The test is performed by laying the marked sheet of paper over a wire mesh or metal sheet and covering it with a film of thin plastic. The wire mesh or metal sheet is charged up with electricity and the charge is transferred to the paper and plastic film. When fine black powder is shaken over the plastic film, some of it sticks to the charged surface. It sticks more where there are any impressions in the surface and therefore reveals what was written on the sheet above it. If a note has been altered after it

In the ESDA test, the document is placed face up on the instrument and covered with a thin film. The film is then charged with electricity.

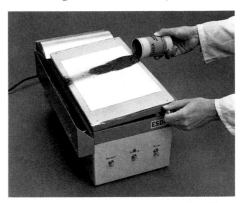

A fine powder is poured over the film until a clear image of the words appears.

was written and torn off the pad, there will be differences between the document itself and the impressions revealed by the ESDA test.

Chemical analysis

Forensic scientists are frequently called upon to analyse unknown substances found at the scene of a crime or in the course of a police inquiry. They may be substances that the police suspect to be poisons or drugs. There are now methods that can analyse and identify the tiniest traces of a chemical.

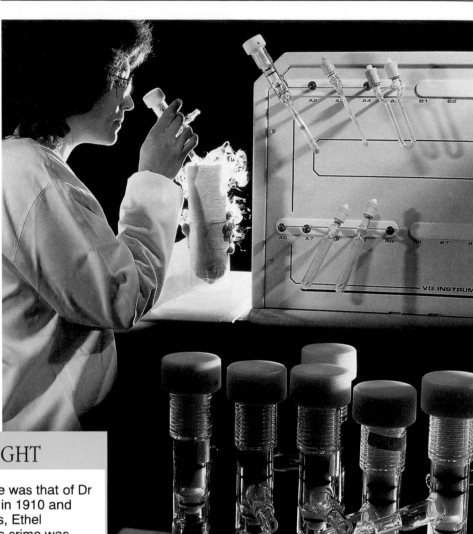

A scientist prepares samples to be tested in a mass spectrometer.

HISTORY SPOTLIGHT

Perhaps the most famous poisoning case was that of Dr Crippen, who poisoned his wife, Belle, in 1910 and fled across the Atlantic with his mistress, Ethel LeNeve, on-board the SS Montrose. His crime was discovered and detectives were waiting to arrest Crippen on his arrival. Dr Crippen was the first criminal to be caught by the use of radio.

Dr Crippen and Miss Le Neve (centre) are arrested.

Throughout most of recorded history, poison has been used by people who were impatient to inherit the wealth, property or power of their superiors or older relatives. Personal advancement by poisoning was so common that poison became known as 'inheritance powder'. Kings, queens and other high-ranking people in history feared the attentions of the poisoner so much that they often employed food tasters to check that meals were free from poison. Food-tasting for an unpopular king could be a fattening but hazardous occupation! As 'ordinary' people acquired more wealth during the 19th century, poisoning became even more widespread. The trials of poisoners were widely reported in the newspapers of Victorian England. Poisoning was common well into the 20th century.

People are rarely poisoned deliberately nowadays because scientists have become so good at detecting all sorts of chemicals. Poisons work by interrupting or damaging the body's natural workings. Their effects may give away their presence, but sometimes chemical analysis is the only way of discovering them.

Scientists can only identify an unknown chemical by splitting it up into a series of

Inside a mass spectrometer

The mass spectrometer separates out heavy atoms, using a magnetic field. This allows the scientist to work out what the original sample was made from.

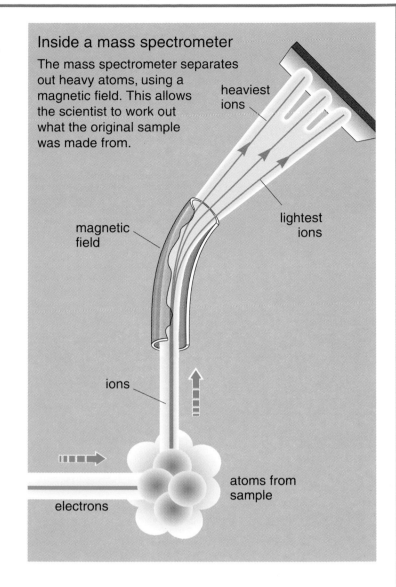

heaviest ions

lightest ions

magnetic field

ions

electrons

atoms from sample

Liquid chromatography

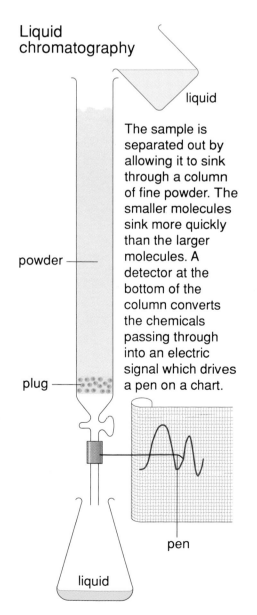

liquid

The sample is separated out by allowing it to sink through a column of fine powder. The smaller molecules sink more quickly than the larger molecules. A detector at the bottom of the column converts the chemicals passing through into an electric signal which drives a pen on a chart.

powder

plug

pen

liquid

simpler compounds. They can do this using chromatography (see pages 22 and 23). These simple compounds can then be split up into even simpler materials by another technique called mass spectrometry. The compound deposited in each chromatography band is placed in the chamber of an instrument called a mass spectrometer.

In the spectrometer, atoms from each chromatography band are bombarded by tiny particles called electrons. They give the atoms an electrical charge. These charged atoms, called ions, are sprayed into a magnetic field. This deflects the ions, or forces them off-course.

The lighter ions are deflected more easily than the heavier ions. The ions therefore become spread out and separated, with the lightest at one end and the heaviest at the other end. Detectors count the number of ions arriving and register where they come from. This tells scientists how many of which atoms were present in the original sample. So, from these basic building blocks, the atoms, scientists can tell which chemical compound was present in each chromatography band. And by putting all the results together from all the bands, the identity of the original sample can be revealed.

Firearms

IT IS AN UNFORTUNATE FACT that more criminals carry firearms now than ever before. Fortunately, firearms specialists are expert at identifying the gun used to fire a bullet and can therefore link a weapon to a particular crime.

A policeman test-fires a gun

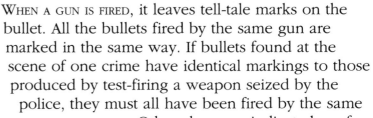

Cartridges and bullets can provide clues. Notice the dent on the cartridge base (far left) and the rifling patterns on the two bullets (far right).

WHEN A GUN IS FIRED, it leaves tell-tale marks on the bullet. All the bullets fired by the same gun are marked in the same way. If bullets found at the scene of one crime have identical markings to those produced by test-firing a weapon seized by the police, they must all have been fired by the same gun. Other clues can indicate how far the weapon was from a victim when the shot was fired, and the direction of the shot.

A bullet has two parts. The front part of the bullet is the metal pellet that is actually fired out of the gun. Behind that there is a charge of gunpowder called the propellant. When a gun's trigger is pulled, a spring-loaded hammer strikes the back end of the bullet with great force, compressing (squeezing) and igniting a small charge called the primer in the bullet's base. The primer in turn ignites the propellant. The energy released by the exploding propellant pushes the metal slug out of the gun through the barrel.

The inside of a gun barrel has a series of grooves called rifling cut in a spiral from one end to the other. Different gun manufacturers use different rifling patterns. Rifling makes the bullet spin. Without rifling, the bullet could topple end over end, making it very inaccurate and reducing its range. A spinning bullet travels straight through the air. The rifling cuts a unique pattern of marks into the bullet and identifies it forever as having been fired by one particular gun.

Cartridge cases, which hold a bullet until it is fired are almost as useful as the bullet itself to a forensic scientist, because they carry the unique marks of the gun's ejector and the firing pin on the hammer. A revolver holds its full cartridges in a revolving chamber. Every time the trigger is pulled, the chamber turns so that a new bullet is in front of the hammer. Spent (used) cartridges cases stay in the chamber until the gun is reloaded. Automatic weapons throw out each spent cartridge case when the gun is fired.

Shotguns have no rifling. The inside of the barrel is smooth, because the shotgun does not fire a bullet. It fires a package of tiny metal balls called shot. The chemical composition of the shot, the propellant and fragments of material in the cartridge called wadding can tell scientists a great deal about the cartridge and the weapon that fired it. When a shotgun is re-loaded, it ejects the empty cartridge cases, so, unless the criminal is incredibly tidy, scientists will have the spent cases to examine.

The fully-loaded chamber of a revolver

HISTORY SPOTLIGHT

THE FIRST HAND-GUNS were developed from small cannon in the Middle East in about the13th century. The earliest recorded examples of police officers using the marks on bullets to solve a crime date back to the 1830s. In 1835, a Bow Street runner (the forerunners of the modern police) called Henry Goddard proved that a bullet said to have been fired by a burglar had in fact been fired by a butler at the house, because marks on the 'burglar's' bullet exactly matched marks on bullets fired by the butler's own gun. Even before this, surgeons had sometimes noticed marks on lead balls fired by muskets. A bullet was first matched to a gun in the modern way, by comparing rifling marks on the bullet to rifling in the gun barrel, in 1889 in France. In that year, Professor Alexandre Lacassagne looked at a bullet taken from a murder victim and compared its markings with the rifling grooves cut into the barrel of a gun found nearby. The two matched and the gun's owner was found guilty of murder.

…ETHER STARTED by …ident or deliberately, …an destroy evidence of another crime. Fire consumes documents, photographs, fingerprints, clothing, furniture, chemicals and most other evidence. But some clues do survive fire.

A charred map

THE FIRST THING a scientist may do on arriving at the scene of a fire is to sniff the air. Even though petrol burns quickly, fiercely and completely, the smell of petrol or other inflammable liquids used to start a fire may still hang in the air after the fire has been put out. Liquids like petrol used in this way are

A fire that seems to have spread through a building more rapidly than normal is immediately suspicious.

Taking samples from the scene of a fire

called accelerants. If the smell of the accelerant can be detected, then traces of the accelerant itself may be detectable in any absorbent materials like wallpaper, plaster, carpets or woodwork. The forensic scientist will take samples of all of these for analysis later in the laboratory.

Chromatography (see pages 22 and 23) is used to split the accelerant into simpler chemical compounds which can be identified more easily. Unlike paper and thin layer chromatography, which are used to analyse liquids, gas chromatography is used to detect and identify vapours. Vapour given off by a bag of remains from the fire is sucked into a flow of 'inert' gas – a gas such as nitrogen, helium or argon which carries the sample gas along but does not react chemically with it. The gas is pumped through a tube packed with a material (fibres or particles) that can absorb the vapour. The different gases present in the mixture are absorbed by the material at different rates and therefore they appear at the other end of the column after different lengths of time. The different gases flow out of the column past a detector which drives a pen on a chart. As each compound appears, the pen registers its arrival by drawing a peak on the chart. Each type of accelerant is composed of a characteristic 'cocktail' of compounds which produce an identifiable chart recording.

HISTORY SPOTLIGHT

THERE WAS NO ATTEMPT to set up an organisation to put out fires until the seventeenth century. After the Great Fire of London in 1666, the capital's businessmen and merchants got together to try to protect themselves from the consequences of fire. By the 1770s, they had formed insurance companies to whom they paid 'premiums'. Money from the premiums was paid to anyone whose business was damaged by fire to help them rebuild their business. To reduce the sums paid out, the insurance companies set up their own fire brigades to put out fires and reduce the damage that had to be paid for. Later, private houses were protected by firefighters too. In time the fire service passed from private companies into the hands of local authorities.

Fighting a fire at the turn of the century

Explosives

WHEN A SCIENTIST is called to the scene of an explosion, it may not be clear whether or not a crime has been committed. The explosion may have been caused accidentally by a gas leak. The scientist's job is to find out what caused it. Forensic scientists are expert at reading the signs left by different types of explosive materials.

The site of a terrorist bomb blast in London

A remote-controlled robot is used by bomb disposal teams to handle suspect items.

THE EFFECT OF A BLAST itself gives the scientist the first clues as to what caused it. A gas blast causes a general pushing effect all round the seat of the explosion. Energy is released throughout the whole cloud almost simultaneously. A bomb blast travels out with immense force from a single point, but it dies away as it goes. The scientist can often tell the type of explosion by the pattern of devastation. Other clues come from tiny fragments of debris that have been flung into the walls and furniture near the seat of the explosion and become buried in them. By measuring how deep they are buried, the scientist can work out how fast they were flying. If the fragments were travelling at a speed of 1,000 metres per second or more, then a bomb is the most likely cause of the explosion.

If the scientist decides that the explosion has been caused by a bomb, the debris is sifted to look for pieces of the bomb. Tonnes of material may be taken away for careful examination in the laboratory. Even the tiniest pinhead-sized fragment can give a clue as to how the bomb was made and detonated. A fragment of printed circuit board may indicate that an electronic timer was used. Pieces of a watch or clock suggest a clockwork timer. An electronic timer could have been set months before, whereas a clockwork timer is only effective over a time delay of several hours at most. This helps the police to narrow down the time period when the bomb was planted and enables them to search for witnesses who were nearby at that particular time.

How do scientists know whether a part of a watch, for example, has come from the bomb and was not an 'innocent' watch unconnected with the bomb? The high temperature flash at the heart of a bomb explosion leaves its mark on the materials closest to the detonation. Scientists look out for this characteristic burning or melting on suspicious items.

HISTORY SPOTLIGHT

THE MODERN HISTORY of explosives began with a Swedish chemist called Alfred Bernhard Nobel (1833-1896). Two explosives called nitrocellulose and nitroglycerin discovered in the 1840s were very powerful but also very dangerous to make and use because they were unstable – they could explode at any moment, particularly if they were handled roughly. In 1867, Nobel discovered that an explosive that was easier to control could be made by soaking liquid nitroglycerin into a fine powder called *kieselguhr*. This is a natural powder produced by the microscopic skeletons of millions upon millions of prehistoric sea creatures called diatoms. Because of this, it is also called diatomaceous earth. Nobel called his new explosive, dynamite. He used the vast fortune he amassed from his discovery of dynamite to establish the Nobel Prizes which are still awarded today for achievements in physics, chemistry, physiology or medicine, literature and peace. An extra award for economics was added in 1969.

Alfred Nobel

Making pictures

SOMEONE WHO SEES a person committing a crime may have a clear picture of the criminal in their head. The police can only make use of what the witness has seen by turning that mental picture into something that everyone can see – a picture of the suspect.

IN THE PAST 50 YEARS or so, the police have used several systems for creating a picture of a suspect. One of the first, called Identikit, was developed by Hugh McDonald in America and introduced by the Federal Bureau of Investigation (FBI) there in the 1950s. It was used by selecting drawings of facial features from a kit containing hundreds of drawings of noses, chins, mouths, ears, eyes, hairlines and other facial features. The separate features were put together in a frame to form a face. The Identikit officer worked alongside the witness. If the witness felt that the nose in the picture was too broad or the eyebrows too thick, the officer could change them until the witness was satisfied that the face resembled that of the suspect.

The major drawback of the Identikit system was that the picture it produced wasn't very

A computer image of a face built up on a human skull. Such images can help to identify bodies.

Photofit pictures can help to track down suspects.

A scientist prepares to build a model of a face based on the cast of a skull.

THE TECHNIQUE OF PLASTIC or facial reconstruction was developed by a Russian professor called Mikhail Gerasimov from earlier work pioneered at the end of the nineteenth century in Switzerland. Gerasimov was an archaeologist and anthropologist. He studied our ancestors, the people who lived in prehistoric times. He used facial reconstruction to produce lifelike models of how prehistoric people may have looked when they were alive. His work came to the attention of forensic scientists in Moscow who wondered if the technique was accurate enough to reconstruct the appearance of more recent unidentified bodies. Gerasimov was asked to reconstruct no less than 12 skulls whose appearance in life was known to the forensic scientists but not to Gerasimov. Each skull was given a number to identify it. Gerasimov had no information about its 'owner's' age, sex, colour or nationality. The experiment was an overwhelming success. All 12 skulls could be identified by comparing Gerasimov's reconstructions with photographs of the heads. As a result, the technique of facial reconstruction was adopted by Russian forensic scientists and Gerasimov became the first director of Russia's Laboratory for Plastic Reconstruction.

lifelike. The Photofit system, devised by Jacques Penry in Britain in 1971, produces a more realistic picture than Identikit because it builds up a picture of the suspect's face from photographs of parts of the face instead of drawings. Sometimes the best result can be obtained by a skilled artist working with the witness. Guided by the witness, the artist makes a lifelike drawing of the suspect.

The latest techniques rely on computer images to build up a facial picture.

Rebuilding faces

IDENTIKIT AND PHOTOFIT, and modern techniques such as Video-fit and E-fit, all try to produce a picture of a living person from a witness's description. Occasionally, the police may have a rather

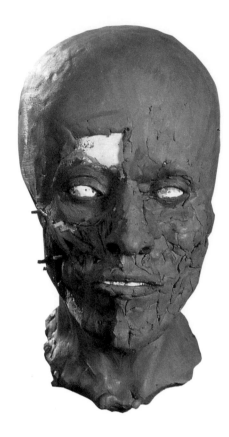

different problem. They may have the tricky task of identifying a person from badly decomposed or burned remains. Dental records can sometimes help (see page 12). If the police have some idea of who the remains may belong to, they may superimpose a photograph of the skull on a photograph of the living person to see if they match. But if the police have no clues as to the person's identity, an extraordinary technique called facial reconstruction or plastic reconstruction is used to recreate the appearance of the living person in the hope that someone will recognise him or her.

The bones of our skull are covered by muscles and skin. Scientists know exactly where the muscles are and how thick they are at each point on a living person's face. They can use this knowledge to reconstruct a dead person's face. They make a plaster cast of the skull of the dead person, and insert wooden pegs into the plaster so that they stick out by the thickness of the flesh at that point on a living person's head. The layers of muscle and skin are then built up in clay until the pegs are just covered. With false eyes, teeth and hair, and realistic skin colouring, the result can be extremely life-like. The reconstructed head is photographed and shown to people or published in newspapers. It has been successful in identifying people on many occasions.

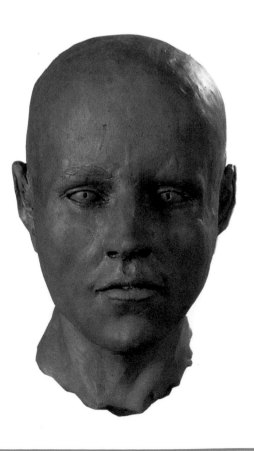

Mind hunters

WHEN POLICE OFFICERS are investigating a serious crime, they often form a mental picture of the person they believe is responsible. Their mental image is a combination of all the facts that are known about the person – age, height, weight, colouring, style of clothes, type of vehicle and so on. In recent times a new and powerful factor has added even more detail to this image. It is called a psychological profile. The

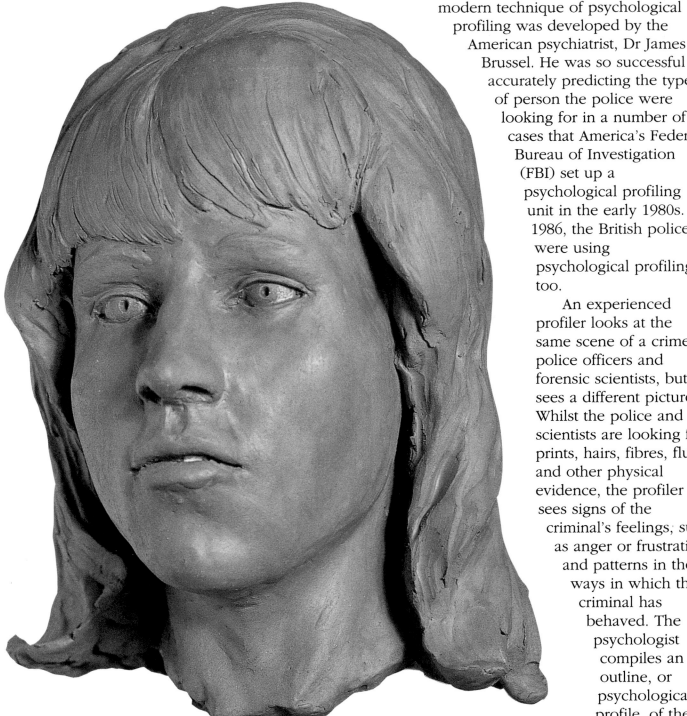

modern technique of psychological profiling was developed by the American psychiatrist, Dr James Brussel. He was so successful in accurately predicting the type of person the police were looking for in a number of cases that America's Federal Bureau of Investigation (FBI) set up a psychological profiling unit in the early 1980s. By 1986, the British police were using psychological profiling too.

An experienced profiler looks at the same scene of a crime as police officers and forensic scientists, but sees a different picture. Whilst the police and scientists are looking for prints, hairs, fibres, fluids and other physical evidence, the profiler sees signs of the criminal's feelings, such as anger or frustration, and patterns in the ways in which the criminal has behaved. The psychologist compiles an outline, or psychological profile, of the criminal. The profile may be very detailed indeed, including even the sort of job the person may have and the style of clothes he is most likely to wear. The profile enables the police to identify the most likely suspects. If psychologists can provide the police with a sufficiently detailed profile, there may be only one person that the police have interviewed who fits the profile in every respect. A computer can pick him out of its memory in seconds (see pages 42 and 43).

HISTORY SPOTLIGHT

THE FIRST PERSON to develop ways of analysing a person's personality was the Austrian psychiatrist Sigmund Freud (1856-1939). He showed how someone's early experiences, memories, feelings and family relationships might affect their personality and behaviour. One of the methods that Freud used to reveal the reasons why people behave in certain ways and what the causes of nervous illnesses might be was to analyse their dreams. This and other techniques that he developed became known as psychoanalysis.

Using computers

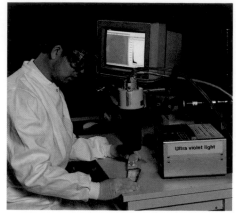

A scientist uses a computer to look at fingerprints on a knife.

SOLVING A CRIME is a process of collecting and sorting information and using it to identify the criminal. The computer's ability to process large amounts of information very quickly has made it an increasingly important aid in the modern business of crime-fighting.

COMPUTERS CAN DO MORE than merely store information and find it again quickly. They can be programmed to process or analyse the information held in their electronic memory. This ability has speeded up fingerprint identification. Before the computer age, fingerprints found at the scene of a crime had to be identified by someone comparing the unknown prints to each set of prints already held on file. One crime in 1961 resulted in six fingerprint officers spending six months comparing a print found at the scene of the murder with prints held on file. Nowadays fingerprint identification can be done much more quickly by computer, with a skilled fingerprint specialist making the final confirmation.

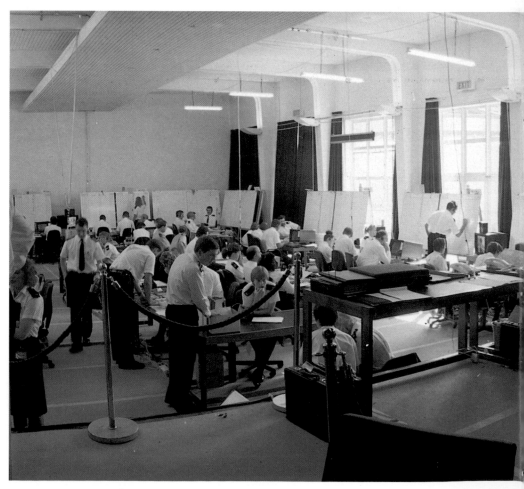

Computers play a key role in handling information received in the incident room set up after a serious crime.

A major police inquiry into a serious crime is an enormously complicated operation. The statements taken from witnesses and many other people who are indirectly linked with the crime may contain thousands upon thousands of individual pieces of information. All the clues necessary to solve the crime and identify the criminal may be buried in these statements, but it is very difficult and time-consuming to sift through the irrelevant information to find the few useful facts amongst the irrelevant material. However, computers can analyse information very quickly indeed. If, for example, the police believe that the person responsible for a crime may have lived or worked in a particular district of a town, may have access to printing equipment and may be a keen sports fan, the computer can search through every statement in its memory and find all the references to the people who satisfy these factors.

In many professions and industries automation is feared as a way of replacing people with machines. But computers will never replace the police officer and the forensic scientist, because computers can only do what they are programmed to do. Their value is that they can do very simple things extremely quickly. The inventiveness and versatility of the police officer and the forensic scientist will always be needed to develop and prove new theories and techniques. Computers and computer-controlled equipment are merely tools that supply vital information quickly to police officers and leave scientists free to advance their work more rapidly than ever.

THE FIRST COMPUTERS built in Britain during the 1940s were massive machines with up to 1,500 glass 'vacuum tubes' or valves weighing several tonnes. They were extremely unreliable and needed a team of highly trained people to keep them running and to interpret their results. And the computers had to be rewired for each new problem they tackled. Computers like these were far too slow, cumbersome and unreliable to be of any practical help to police officers and forensic scientists. It was the development of small, fast and powerful computers in the 1970s that enabled the power of the computer to be brought to bear on the information storage and processing problems of crimefighting.

Glossary

Anthropometry a system for identifying people by measurements taken from their body, invented by Alphonse Bertillon.

Autopsy a medical examination of a body after death.

Ballistics the study of guns, rifles, and ammunition.

Chromatography a scientific technique for separating a chemical compound into its simpler constituents by passing it through or over a material that slows down the progress of different substances at different rates.

Dactyloscopy another name for fingerprinting. A system for identifying people by their fingerprints.

Digitiser a system for converting an image such as a fingerprint or a photograph of a person into a code that a computer can store and process.

DNA DeoxyriboNucleic Acid. Long thread-like molecules in the cells of living organisms that control the growth and development of the organism. The genetic code.

Electrophoresis using an electric field to make particles move through a liquid.

Electrostatic electric energy based on the forces between electric charges.

Enzymes protein molecules that stimulate chemical reactions in the body – the chemical processes necessary to digest food for example.

Fraud the crime of deceiving people (telling lies) to gain a dishonest advantage over them.

Graphology the study of handwriting.

Inert gas a gas such as nitrogen used in chromatography to move the sample to be identified through the equipment without reacting chemically with it.

Infrared invisible electomagnetic radiation beyond the red end of the visible spectrum.

Mass spectrometry a scientific technique for separating and identifying atoms and molecules according to their mass.

Narcotic this originally meant a substance that causes sleepiness or unconsciuosness, but today it is also applied to a range of illegal drugs that may not have this effect.

Pathologist a medical specialist in the study of abnormalities and the cause of disease in the human body. It is a pathologist who examines a body and decides what the cause of death was.

Polygraph a lie-detector, a machine used to measure changes in the human body such as skin resistance (affected by sweating), breathing rate and heart rate.

Post mortem after death. Also another name for the autopsy, the after-death or post mortem examination.

Refractive index the power of a transparent material such as glass to bend light. Useful for matching a piece of glass to glass from the scene of a crime.

Toxicology the study of poisons.

Ultra-violet invisible electromagnetic radiation just beyond the blue-violet end of the visible spectrum.

Vapour the gaseous form of a substance that normally exists as a liquid or solid – water vapour for example.

Voice print a graph or picture produced by using a sound to make a trace on a computer screen or a sheet of paper. Sometimes useful for matching a recording of an unidentified voice with a suspect's voice.

Index